SUPER HITS OF 2002

ISBN 0-634-05572-0

HAL•LEONARD®
CORPORATION

7777 W. BLUEMOUND RD. P.O. BOX 13819 MILWAUKEE, WI 53213

Visit Hal Leonard Online at
www.halleonard.com

AIN'T IT FUNNY

FLUTE

Words and Music by
CORY ROONEY and JENNIFER LOPEZ

BRING ON THE RAIN

Words and Music by
BILLY MONTANA and HELEN DARLING

Flute

COMPLICATED

Words and Music by
AVRIL LAVIGNE, LAUREN CHRISTY,
SCOTT SPOCK and GRAHAM EDWARDS

FLUTE

Moderate Pop

ESCAPE

Words and Music by
ENRIQUE IGLESIAS, DAVID SIEGEL,
STEVE MORALES and KARA DIOGUARDI

Flute

HERE IS GONE

Words and Music by
JOHN RZEZNIK

FLUTE

HERO

Words and Music by ENRIQUE IGLESIAS,
PAUL BARRY and MARK TAYLOR

Flute

A MOMENT LIKE THIS

Flute

Words and Music by
JOHN REID and JORGEN KJELL ELOFSSON

A NEW DAY HAS COME

Words and Music by
STEPHAN MOCCIO and ALDO NOVA

FLUTE

ONLY HOPE
From the Warner Bros. Motion Picture A WALK TO REMEMBER

FLUTE

Words and Music by
JONATHAN FOREMAN

ONLY TIME

Words and Music by ENYA,
NICKY RYAN and ROMA RYAN

Flute

SK8ER BOI

Words and Music by
AVRIL LAVIGNE, LAUREN CHRISTY,
SCOTT SPOCK and GRAHAM EDWARDS

FLUTE

Lively Rock

SOAK UP THE SUN

FLUTE

Words and Music by
JEFF TROTT and SHERYL CROW

SUPERMAN
(It's Not Easy)

Words and Music by
JOHN ONDRASIK

FLUTE

WASTING MY TIME

Words and Music by
DANNY CRAIG, DALLAS SMITH,
JEREMY HORA and DAVE BENEDICT

FLUTE

WHEREVER YOU WILL GO

Words and Music by
AARON KAMIN and ALEX BAND

FLUTE